PICTURE THE ALPHABET

An Alphabet Look and Find Book

This book is dedicated to
Max, Stacie, Brad, Tom and Adam.
I love you all dearly. Now go clean your rooms.

A

B

C

By Cathy Witbeck

PICTURE THE ALPHABET

An Alphabet Look and Find Book

By Cathy Witbeck

Text and illustrations copyright @2023 by Cathy Witbeck

All rights reserved, including the right of reproduction in whole or in part in any form.

Library of Congress number - 2023905637
ISBN - 978-1-7322626-6-9

For contact information go to http://www.calicobarnbooks.com

The illustrations in this book were first sketched, then printed digitally

Printed and bound in the United States of America   August 2023

Picture the alphabet,
What do you see?
It's like looking for treasure.
Come hunting with me.

Search for mini doodles,
Each page has three.
They are good hide and seekers.
Don't you agree?

* At the end of the book there's an answer key.

Aa

Alligator arm wrestles an annoyed alien.

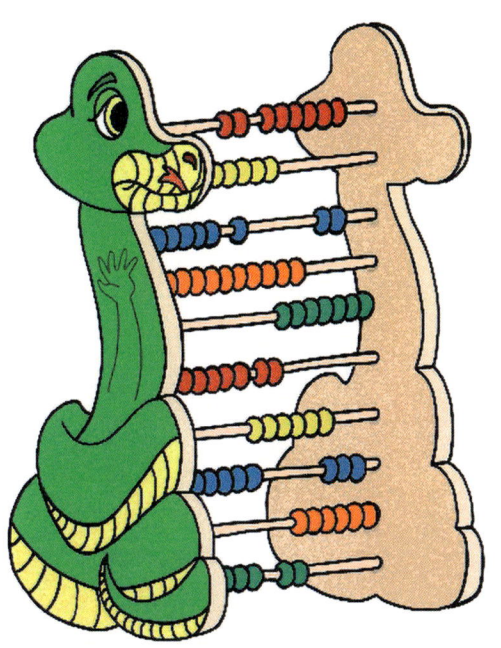

Anaconda
Abacus

Aardvark
Armor

Anchor

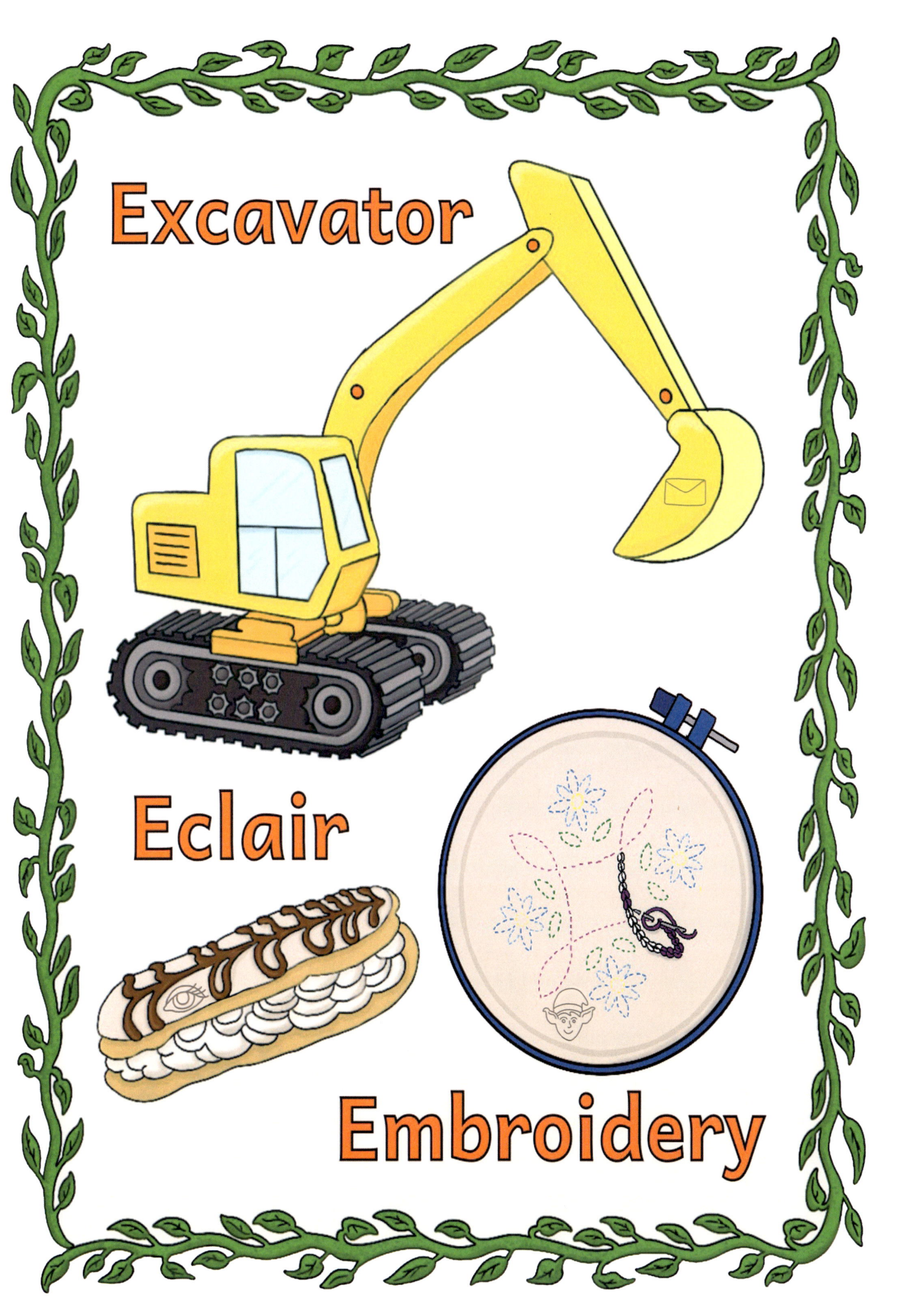

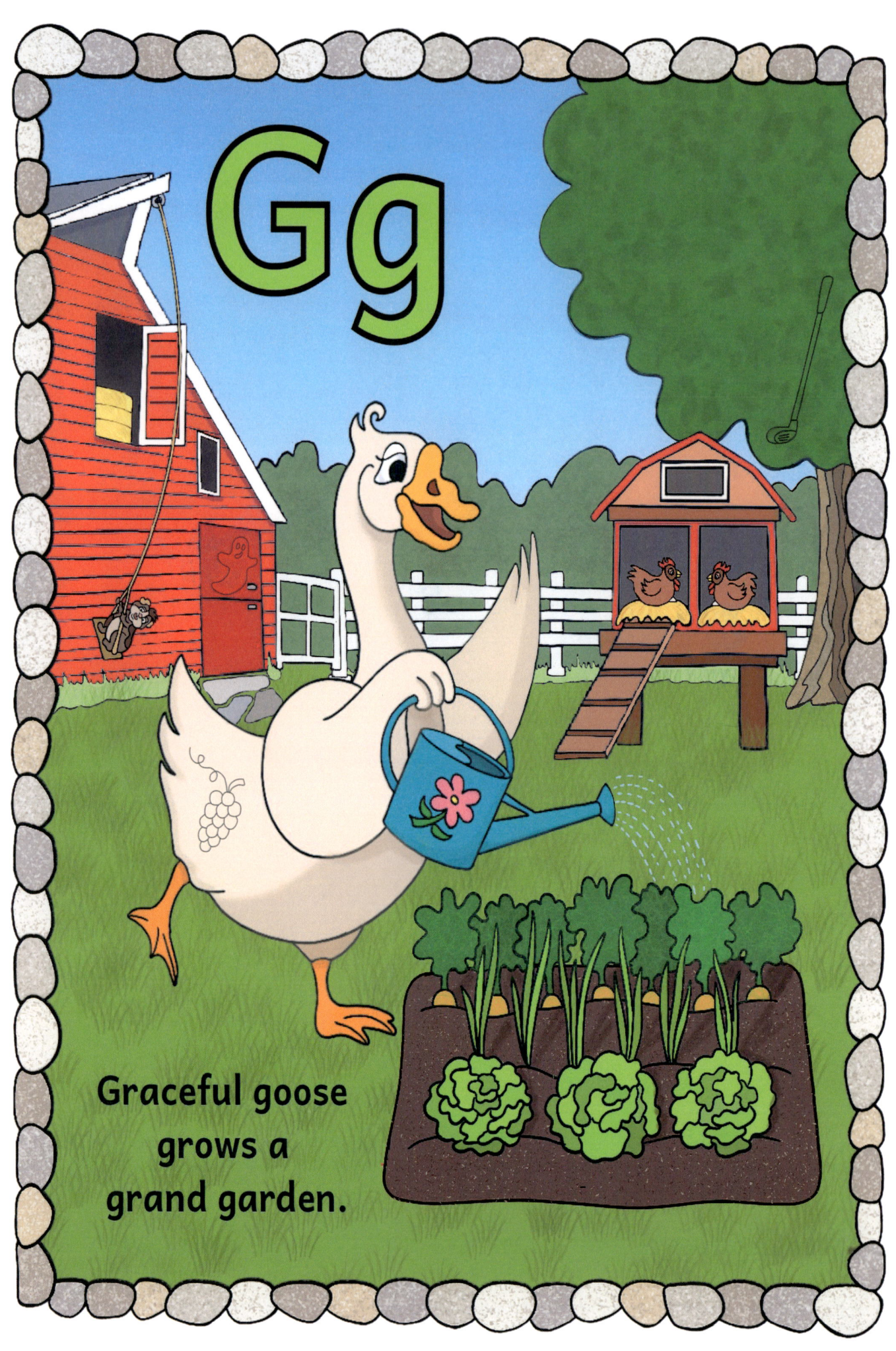

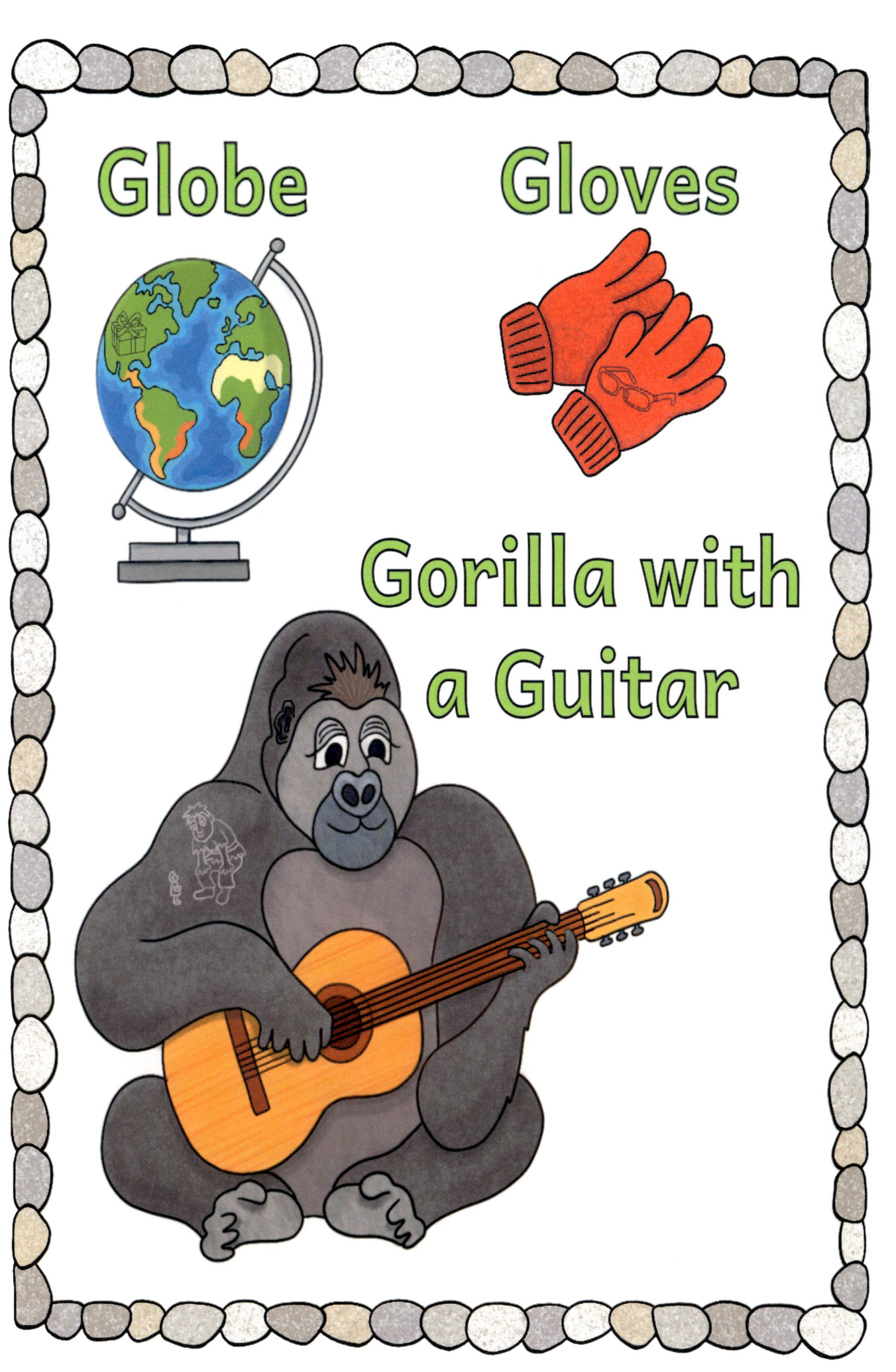

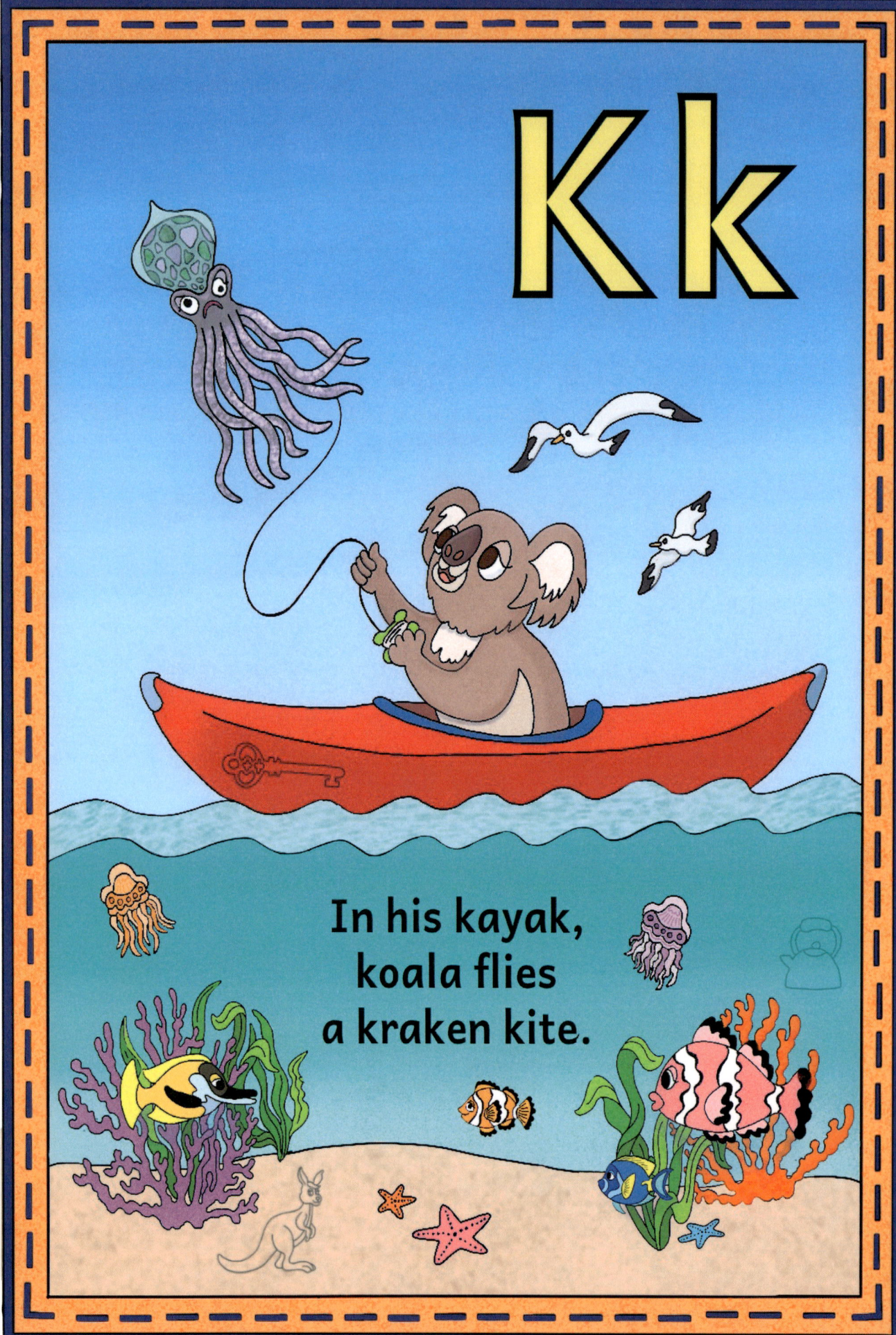

Monsieur mouse makes the most marvelous muffins.

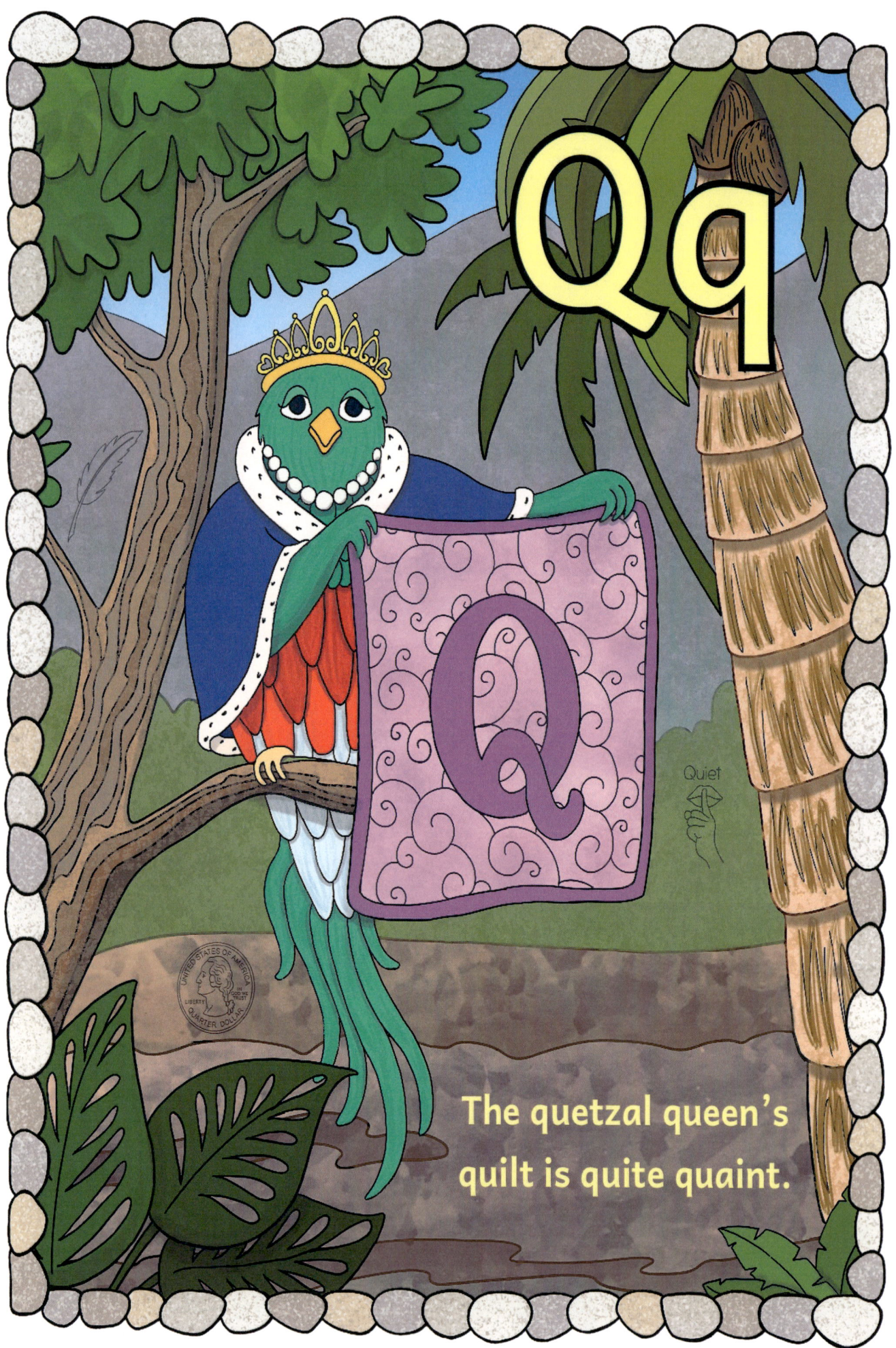

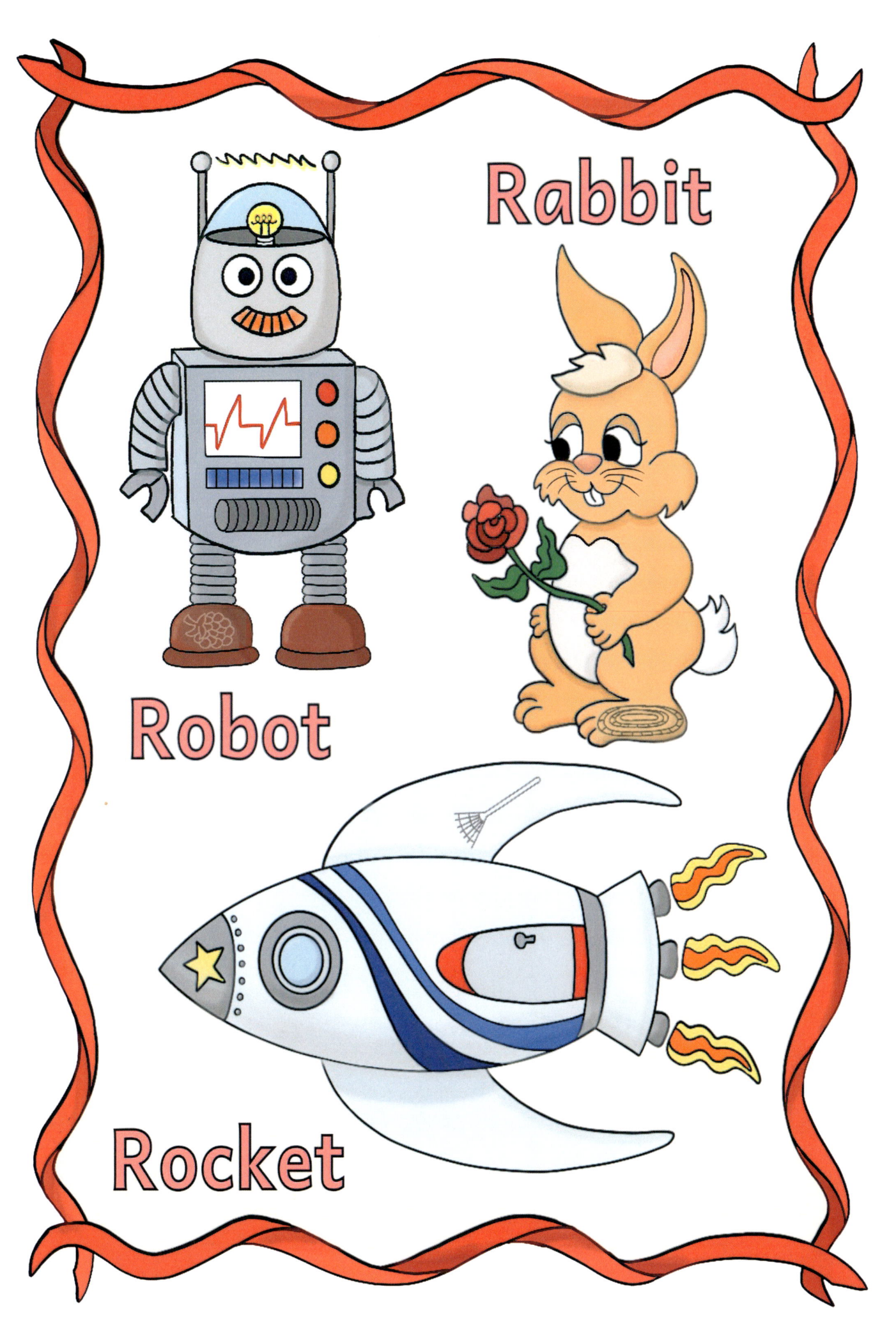

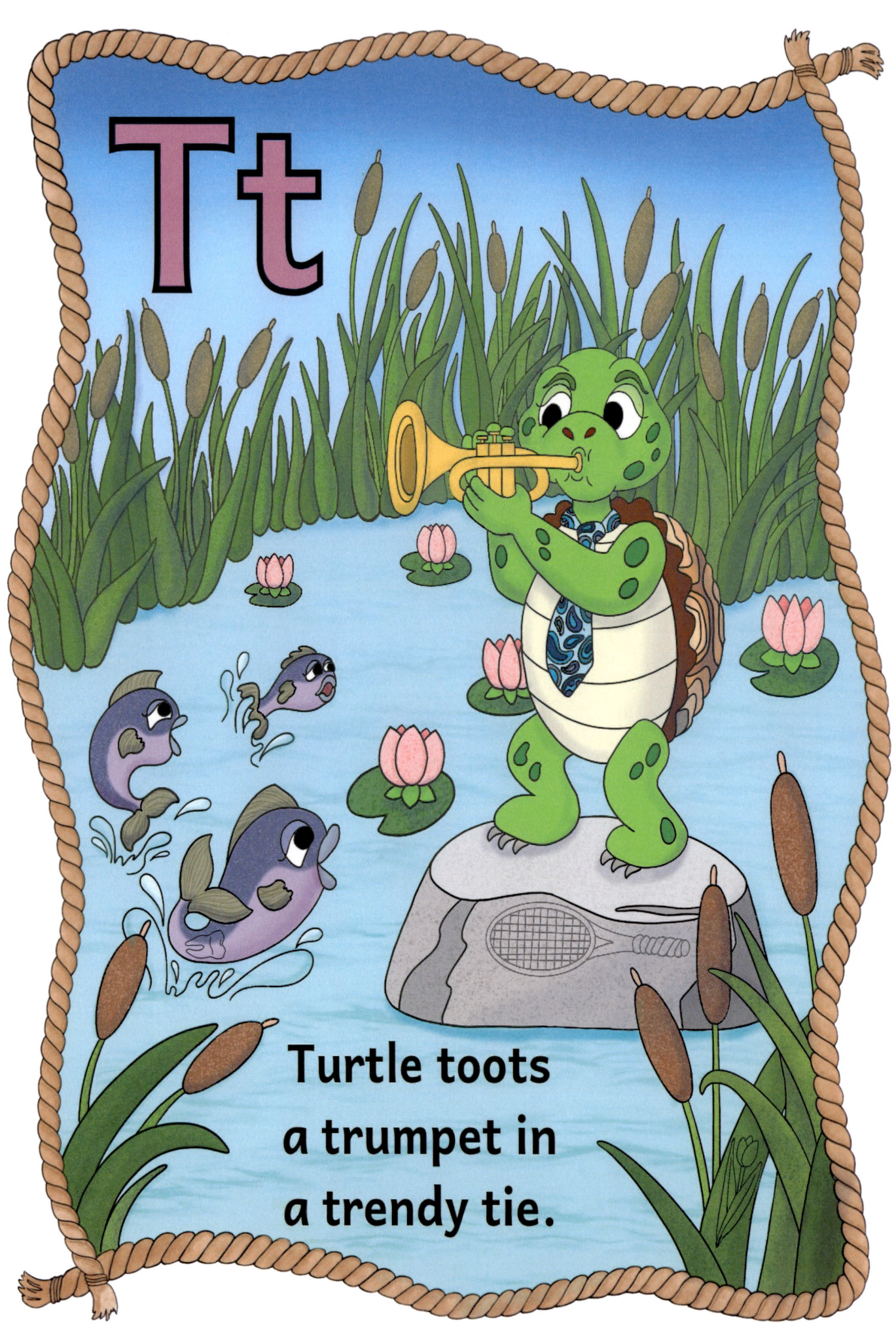

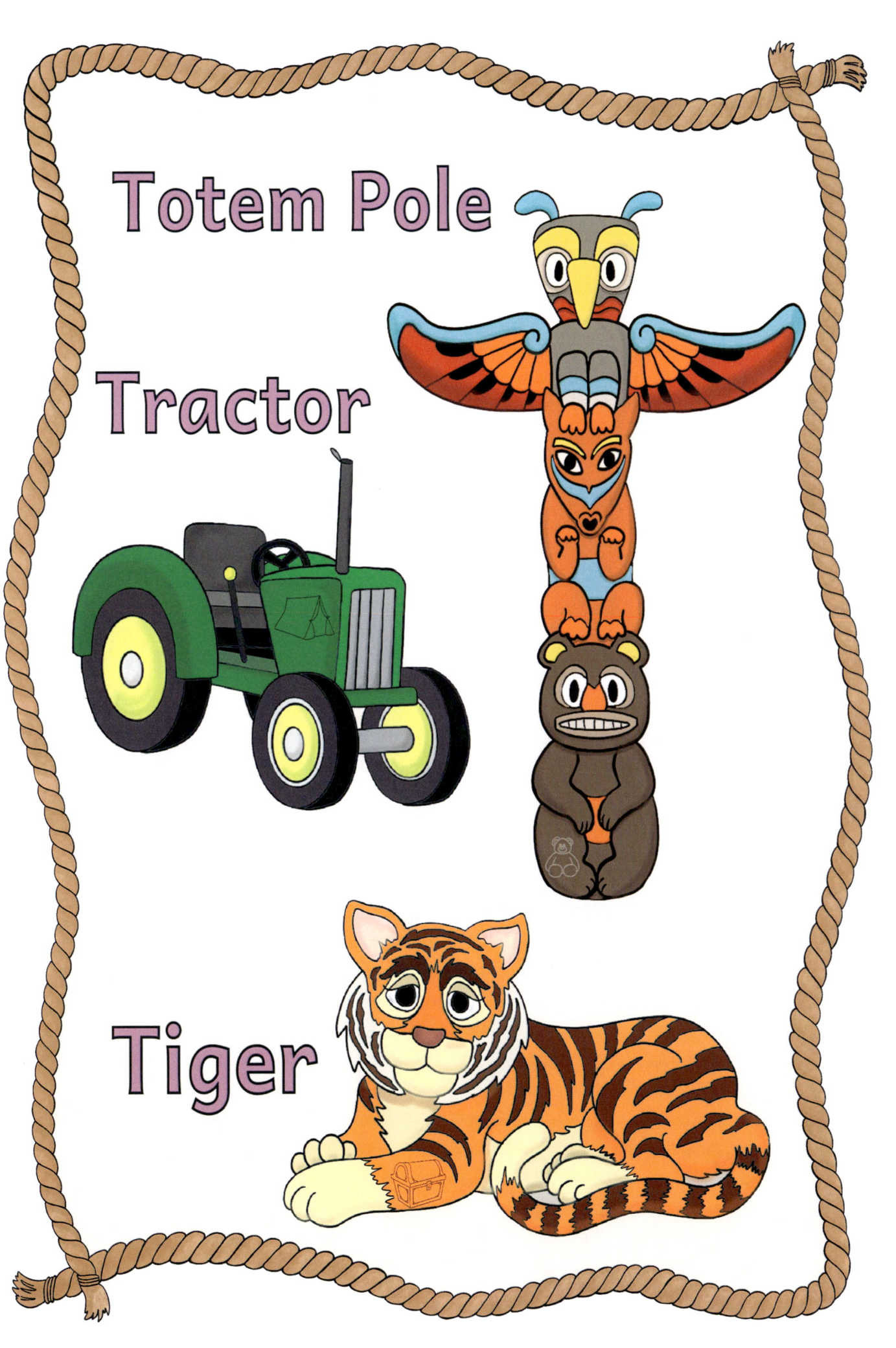

A urial playing a ukulele on a unicycle is unusual in Urbania.

Uu

UFO

Unicorn

Urn

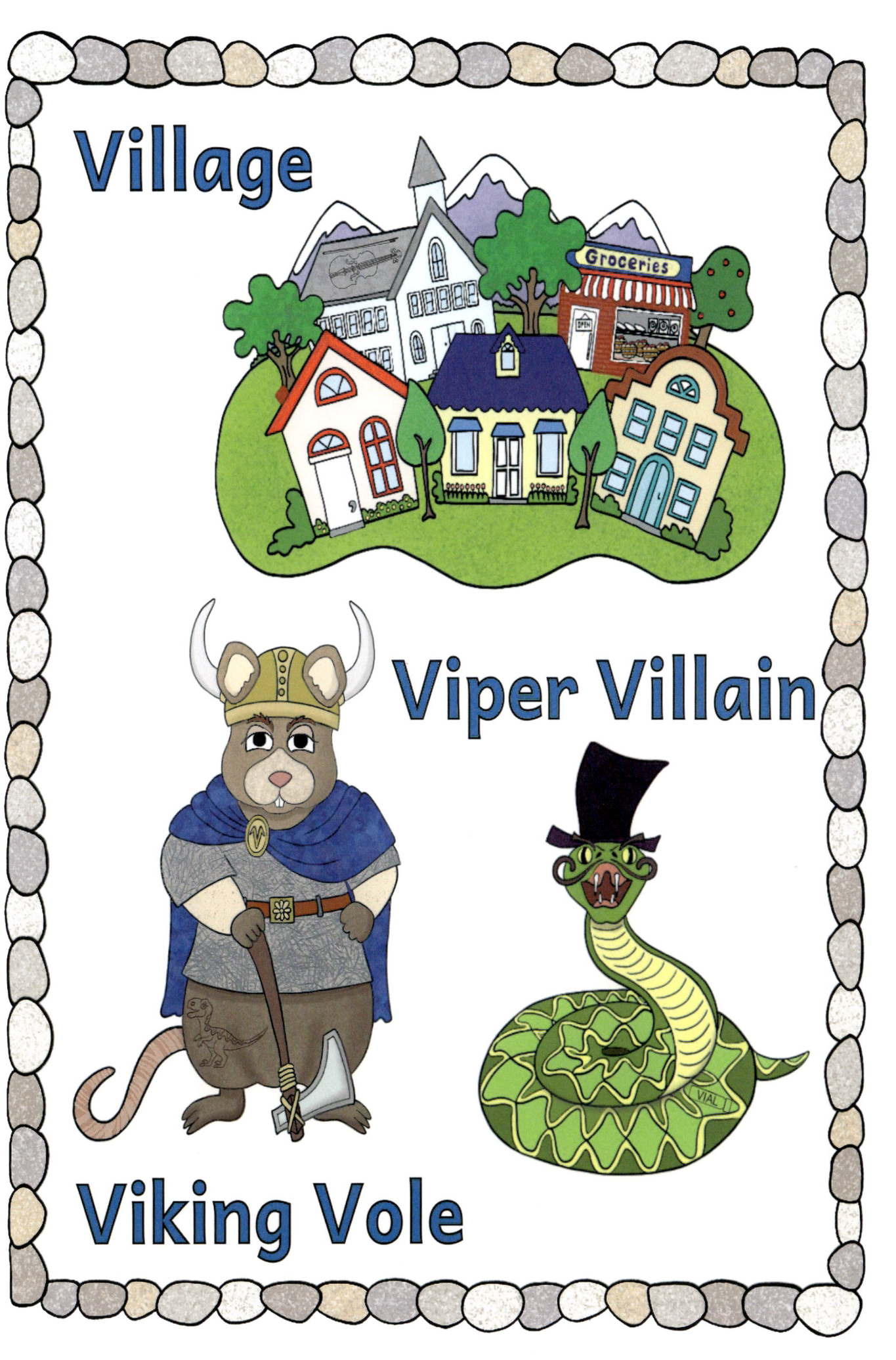

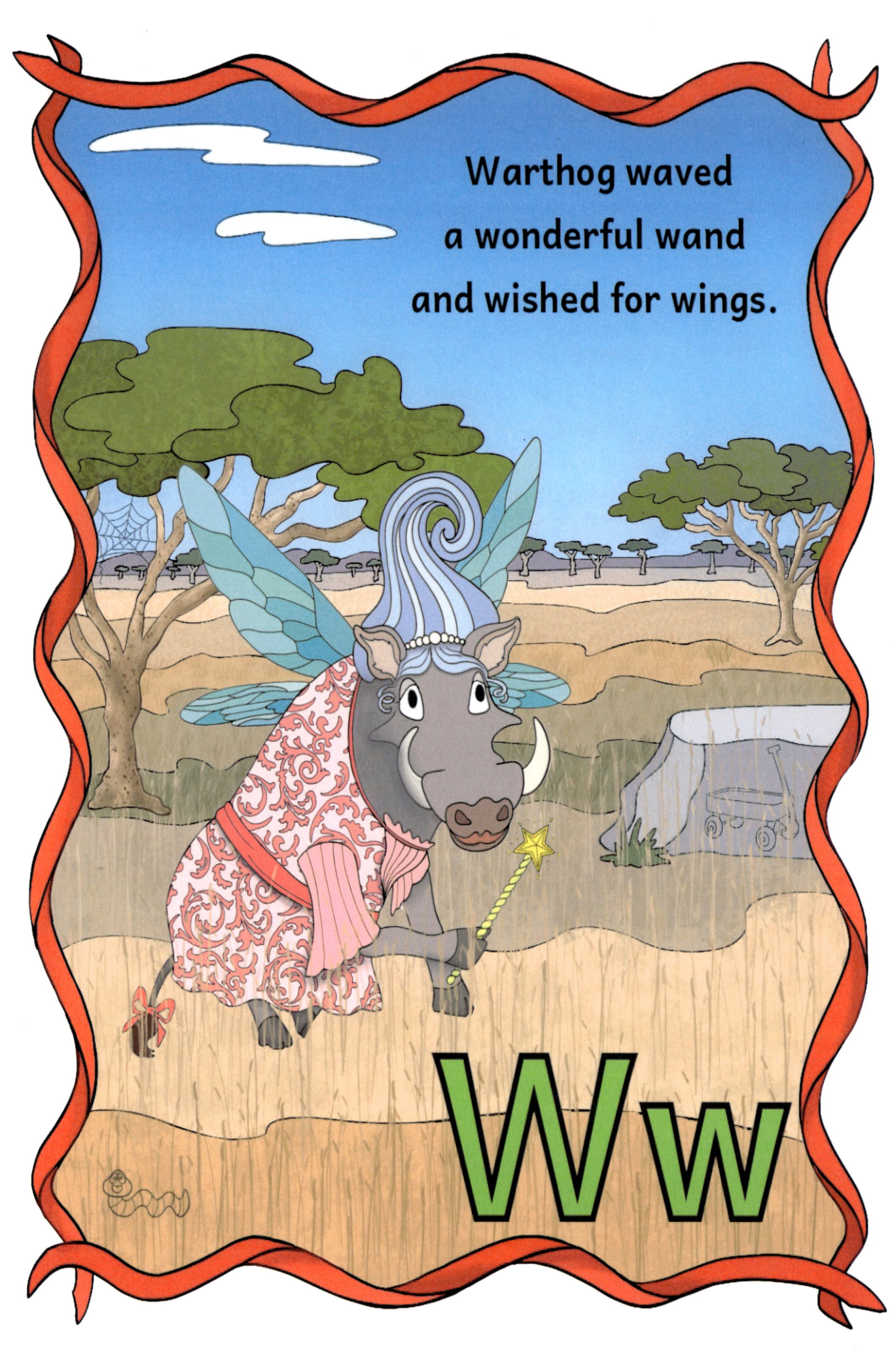

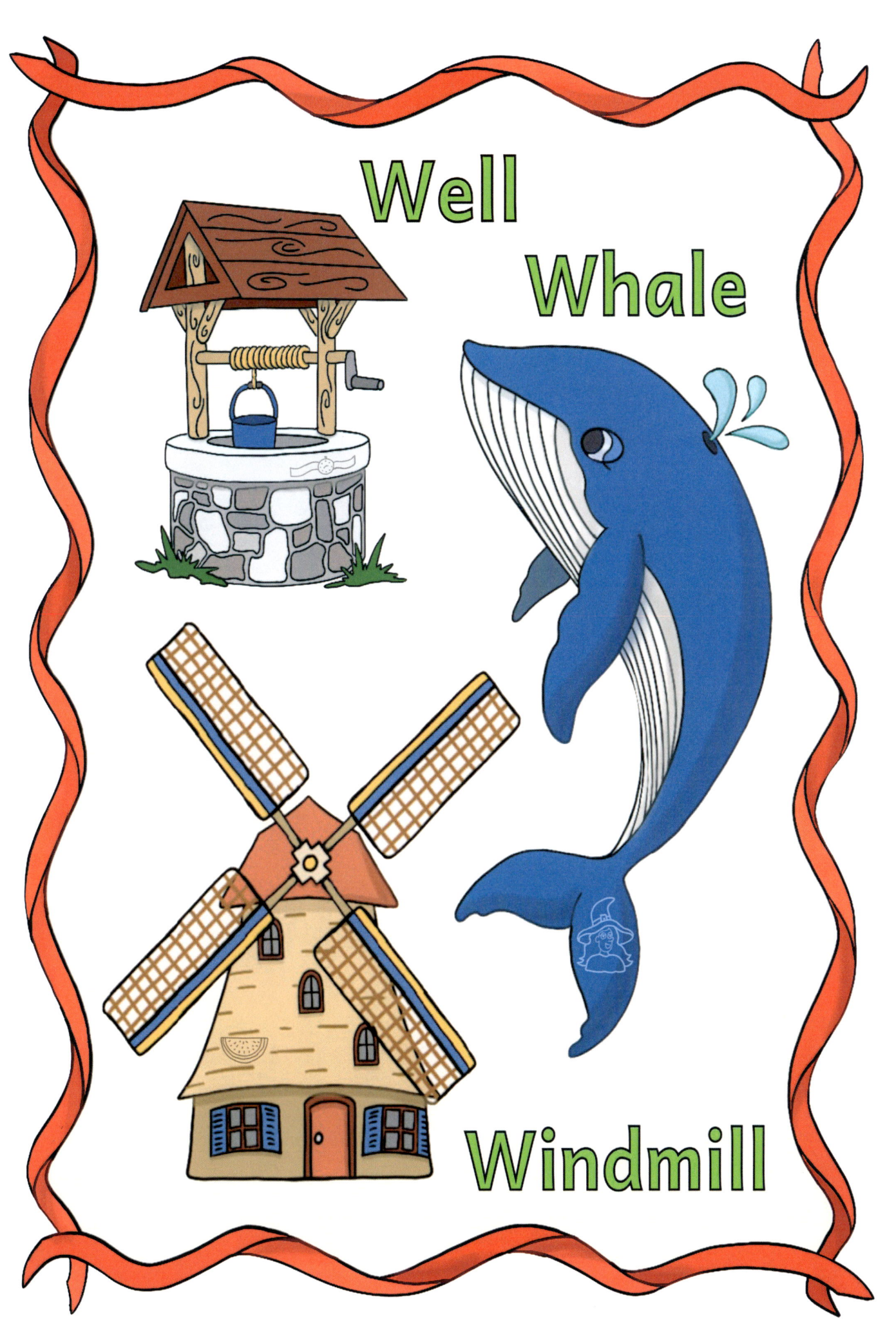

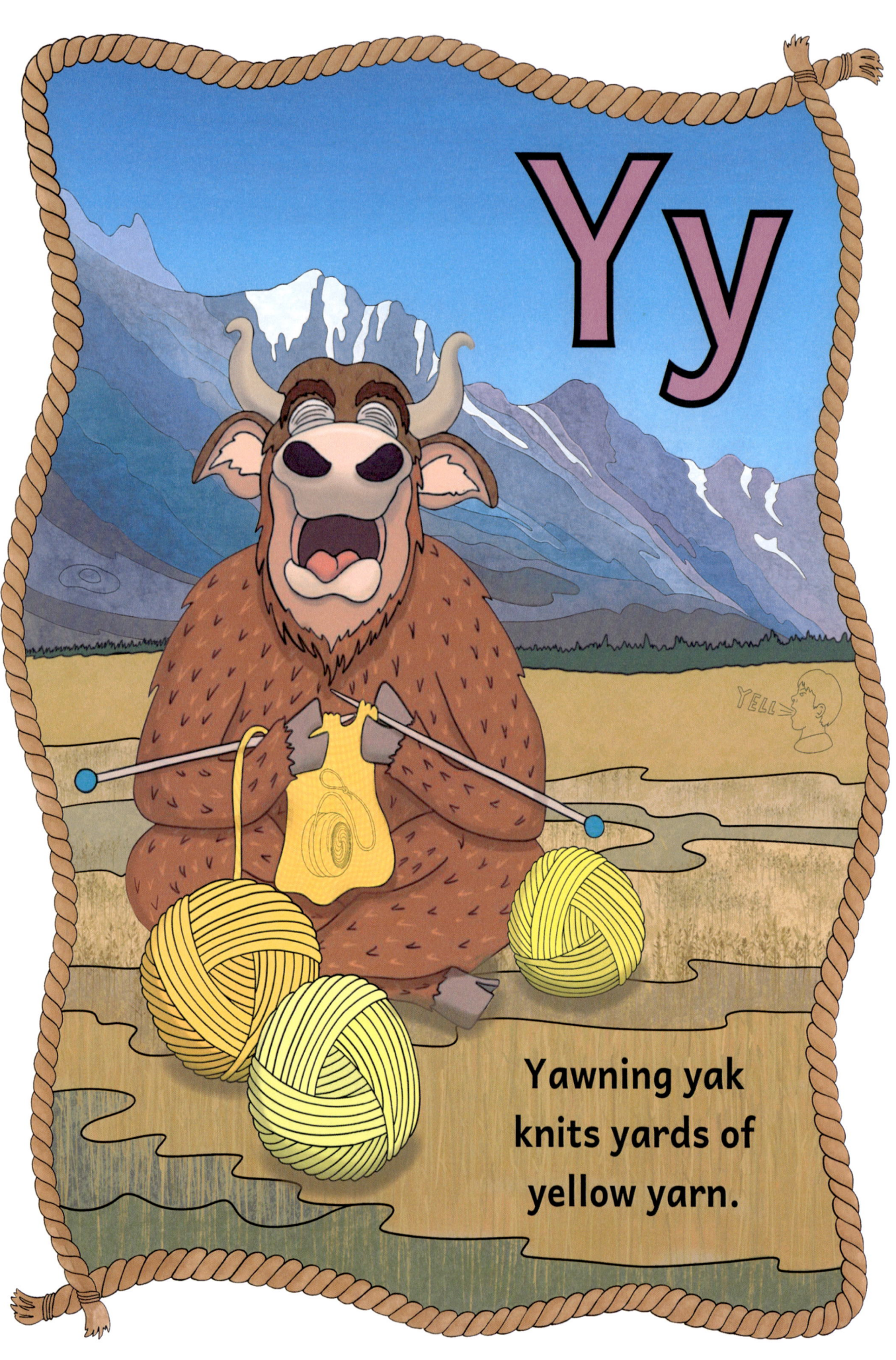

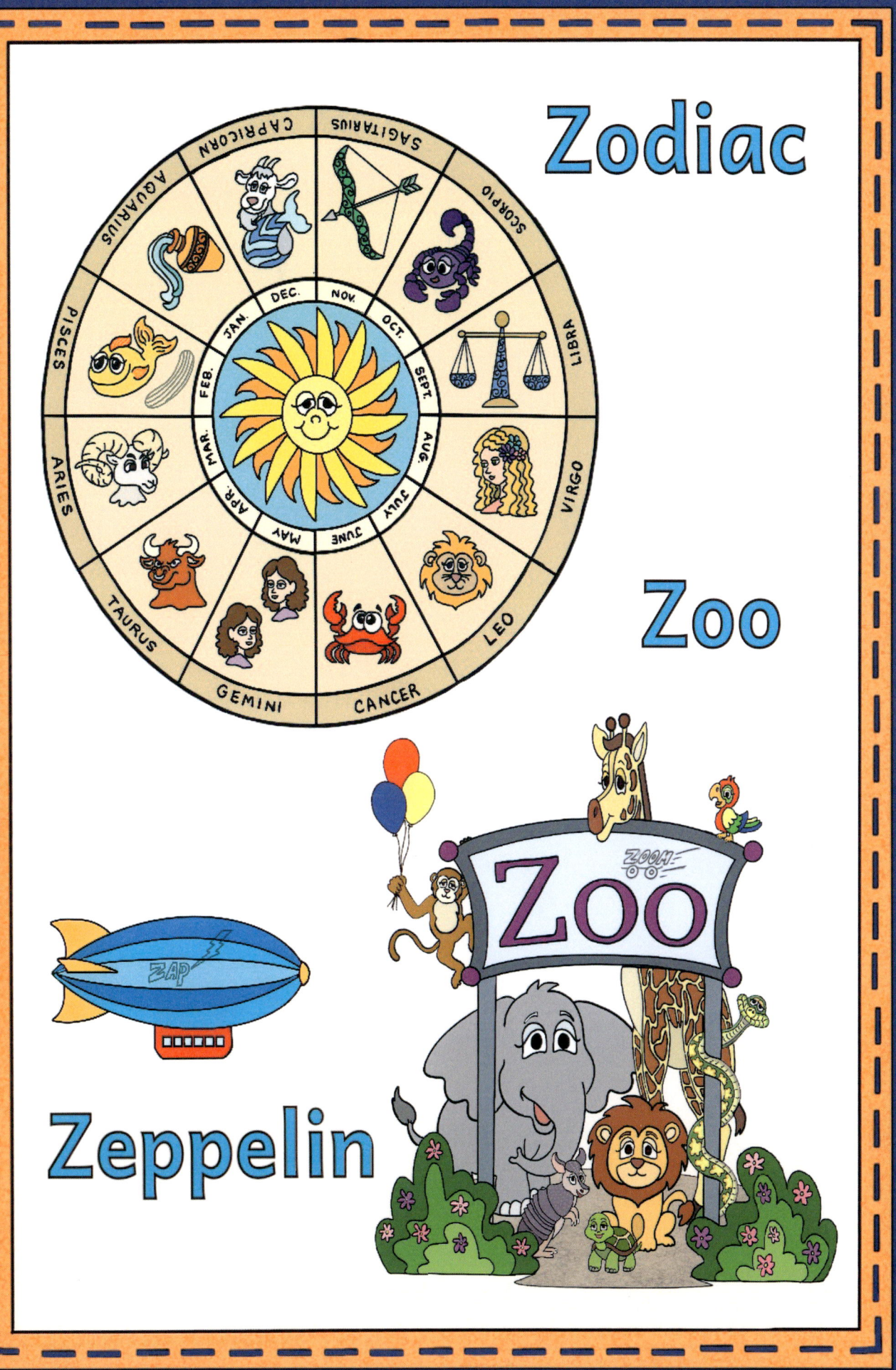

Did you find all the hidden objects?

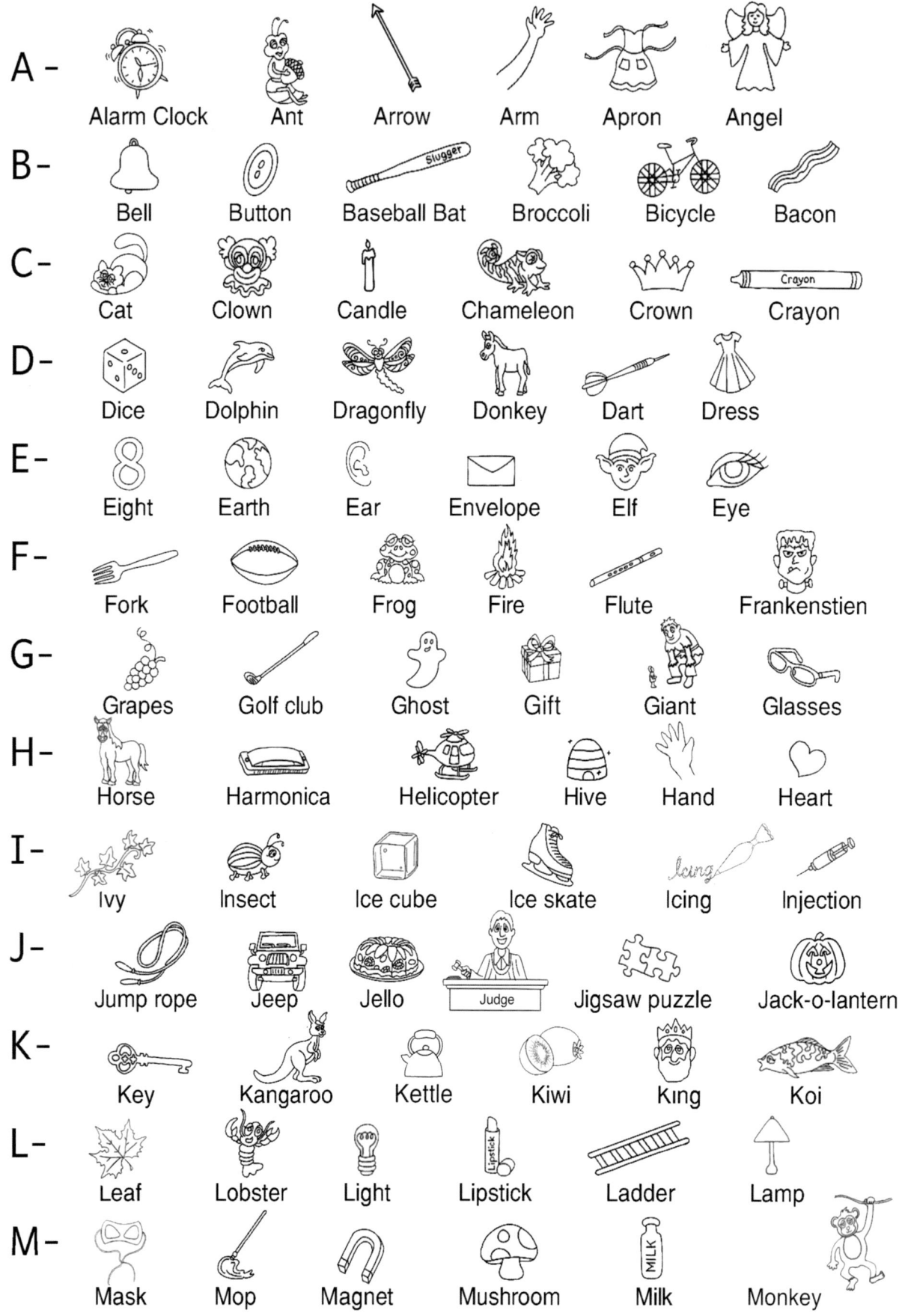

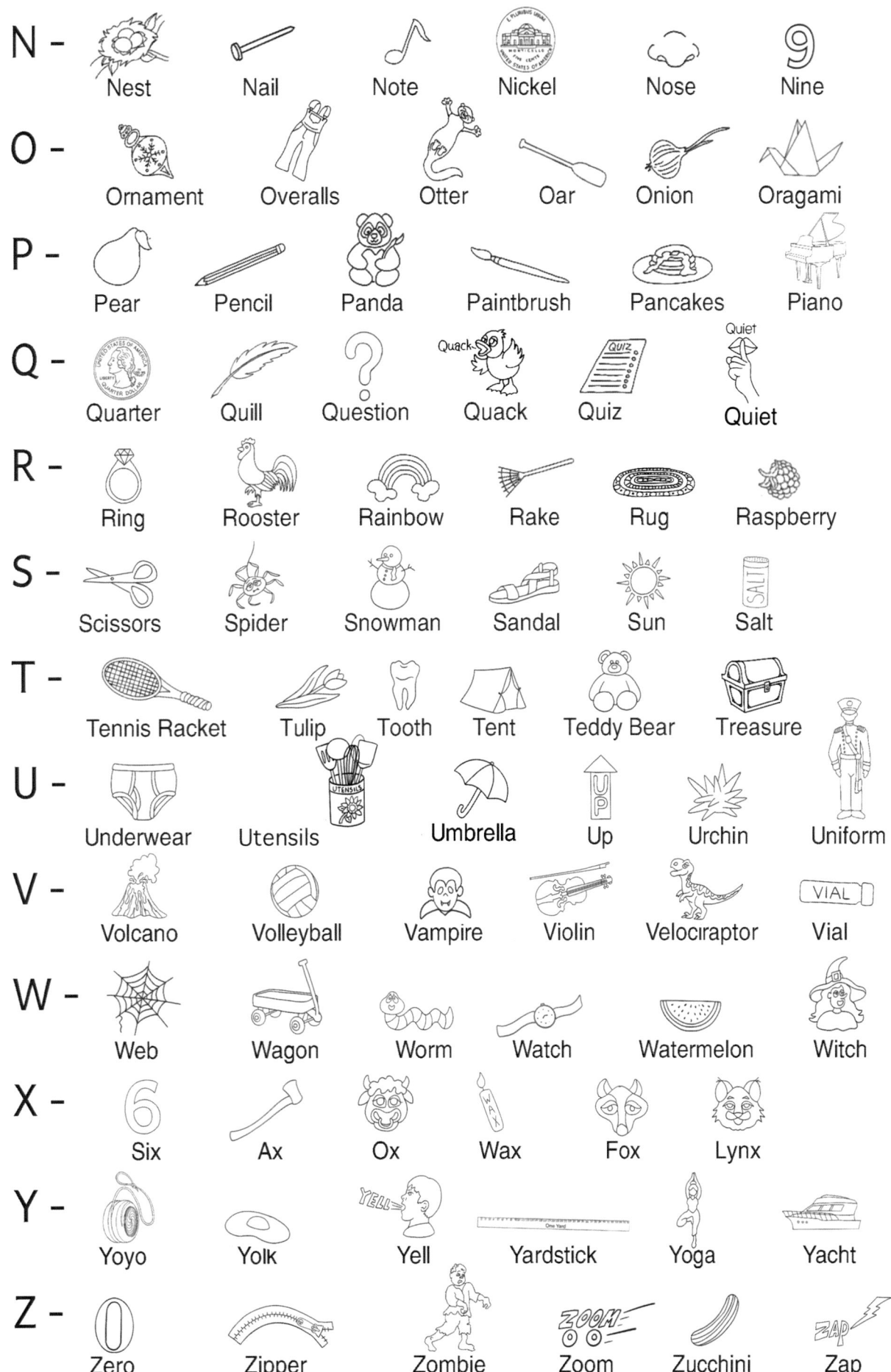

In Case You Were Wondering . . .

Aardvark - a nocturnal burrowing animal in Africa that eats ants and termites.

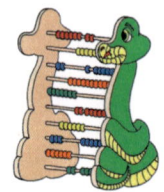

Abacus - A device built for counting or making calculations using beads that slide along rods.

Junk - A type of ancient Chinese sailing ship.

Kraken - An enormous legendary sea monster supposedly inhabiting the coastal waters of Norway.

Lemur - A noctural primate that looks like a monkey, but isn't. It lives in the trees in Madagascar.

Narwal - An arctic marine whale with a long spiraled tooth.

Numbat - A small marsupial witha a long sticky tongue for eating termites.

Quetzal - A large brightly colored bird with long tail feathers in Central America.

Totem Pole - A wooden pole with symbolic images beautifully carved and painted on it.

UFO - An unidentified flying object.

Urn - A large hollow vase with a base.

Urial - An upland wild sheep. Males have a beard from neck to chest.

Vole - A small mouselike rodent, with a wider body, shorter tail and smaller eyes and ears.

Xantus - A midsized hummingbird with an iridescent green throat.

Xenopus - An African clawed frog that is semi-aquatic.

Xerus - A ground squirrel from Africa that looks like a prairie dog.

Yeti - A legendary creature of the Himalayas also known as the Abominable Snowman.
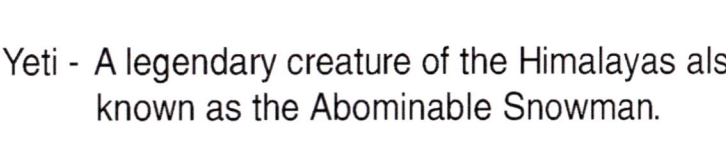

Yurt - A round portable tent used as a home by nomadic people in central Asia.
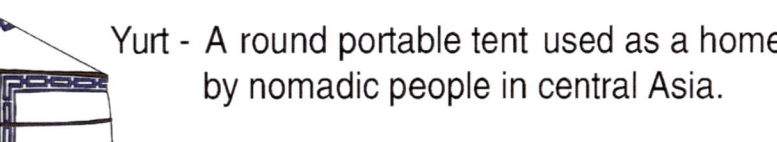

Zamboni - A machine used on a skating rink to smooth the ice with hot water.
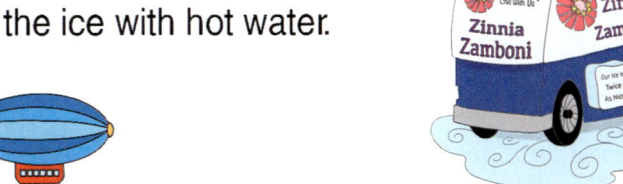

Zeppelin - Also known as an airship, it is a lighter-than-air craft that uses gas to lift it.

Zodiac - The zodiac is a collection of twelve constellations. Each has been assigned the form of an animal or a human.

If you enjoyed

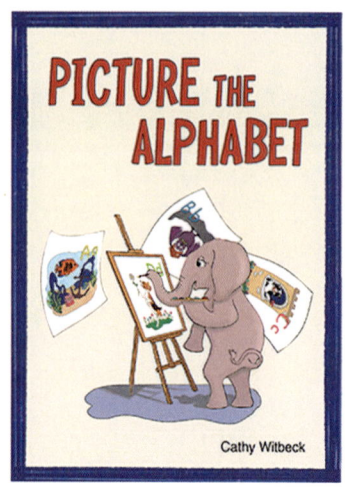

You might enjoy
Learning about Ukrainian Easter eggs

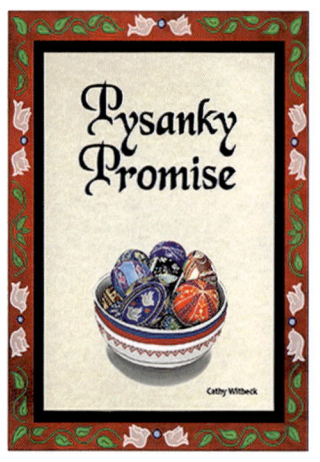
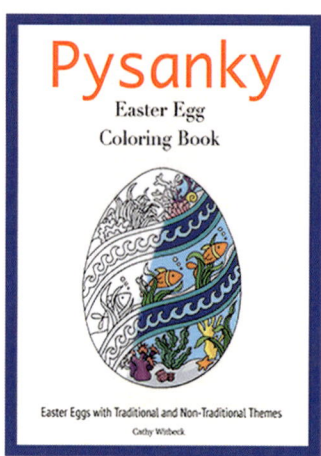

or

Building a Fairy Village

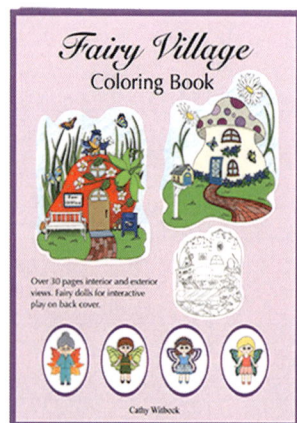

Available on Amazon, Barnes and Noble, & Other fine retailers

Cathy Witbeck is an author-Illustrator who grew up on a ranch in Canada near the Rocky Mountains. Transplanted to the USA, she now lives near the Wasatch Mountains in Utah. She loves to read, write, paint and make Ukrainian Easter eggs, not necessarily in that order. Picture books, family gatherings and ice cream make her happy. She is totally addicted to Chick-Fil-A and mildly obsessed with cows.

You can find books, free printable paper dolls, and a link to her Zazzle website, Calico Barn Designs at www.calicobarnbooks.com.

www.ingramcontent.com/pod-product-compliance
Lightning Source LLC
Chambersburg PA
CBRC091201070526
44583CB00008B/175